# Contents

...sor
...arp

Front cover photograph courtesy of Allsport UK Ltd. All other photographs by Norman Foster.

Illustrations by Tim Bairstow and Ron Dixon of Taurus Graphics.

*Note*   Throughout the book archers and officials are referred to individually as 'he'. This should, of course, be taken to mean 'he or she' where appropriate.

# Introduction

When watching archery for the first time, people often get the impression that it would be too difficult for them because they would not have the strength to pull a bow. This is not the case, because bows are made in different strengths to suit all types of physique, including that of young children. In fact, there are archers of almost every capability and disability. Blind people, paraplegics and even people with one or no arms are able to enjoy the thrill of sending an arrow through the air to a target.

Archery is truly a sport for all.

## The first step

The first question is usually: 'How do I start?'. One thing you must *not* do is go out and buy some tackle. Archery equipment is very powerful, and potentially lethal. It is vital that you are taught how to use it properly before you begin, so that you do not injure yourself or other people.

Archery has a very fine record of safety, which is built upon and maintained through very strict rules of shooting. For this reason, if no other, it is strongly recommended that newcomers to the sport have proper tuition. This can be obtained at your nearest archery club. No matter where you live, there will be a club within a few miles; or you can attend archery classes at an Institute of Further Education near you.

Much later, when you are ready, you will be given advice by the coach on which equipment will suit you and where you can buy it. The coach will usually come with you to ensure that you purchase the best – remembering that the best is not necessarily the most expensive.

## Joining a club

At a club, the usual arrangement is that you pay a small fee, between £5 and £10 at the time of writing, for which you get a series of lessons (five or six) from the club coach. All the necessary equipment is supplied free.

At the end of this, if you wish to continue, the sum you have paid is deducted from the membership fee which you will be required to pay when you join. Club membership fees at present range from £10 to £40 per year, and usually include affiliation to the country, regional and national associations.

The governing body of archery in the United Kingdom is The Grand National Archery Society, which will deal with any enquiries you may have. For further information about your nearest archery club, write to the Society at the following address.

The Grand National Archery Society
7th Street
National Agricultural Centre
Stoneleigh
Kenilworth
Warwickshire CV8 2LG

Alternatively, telephone Coventry (0203) 696631.

Obviously, facilities will vary in different parts of the world, so for information about archery outside the United Kingdom, write to the following address.

The Secretary General
Fédération Internationale de Tir à l'Arc
Via Cerva 30
20122 Milan
Italy

Apart from a bow and some arrows, an archer's basic requirements are an arm guard, a finger tab and a quiver, and a target at which to shoot.

## Arm guard

The arm guard is a strip of leather or plastic which lies along the inside fore-arm of the bow arm and is secured to the arm with elastic or straps, perhaps with Velcro fastening. Its purpose is to prevent bruising by the bowstring slap (*see* page 26). It is sometimes referred to as a *bracer*; although this is a misnomer, it is one commonly used by archers.

## Finger tab

The finger tab has two functions. Fingers are inserted through the holes, so that the tab is between the fingers and the bowstring while the bow is being drawn. This prevents chafing of the fingers by the bowstring, and allows the bowstring to slide freely off the fingers

during the loose (giving the arrow all possible impetus from the energy stored in the bow when it is drawn).

## Quiver

The quiver is a convenient storage place for arrows, so that they come freely to hand during shooting. It is slung on a belt that is usually worn around the waist. Sometimes, in field archery, the quiver is slung across the shoulders to prevent it from catching on undergrowth.

A ground quiver is a metal frame that stands on three legs on the ground. This is designed to support a bow and to hold arrows not in use on the shooting range.

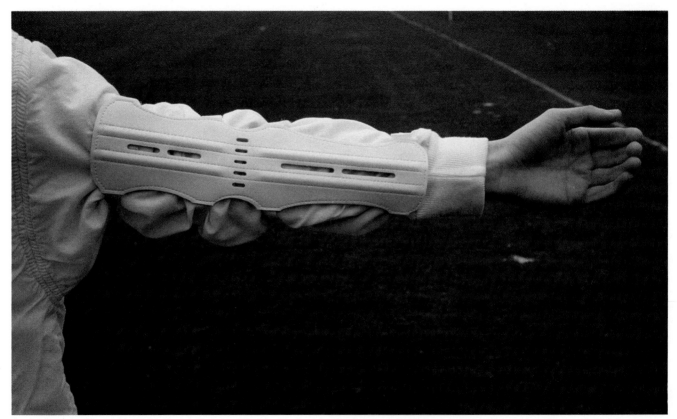

▲ *An arm guard*

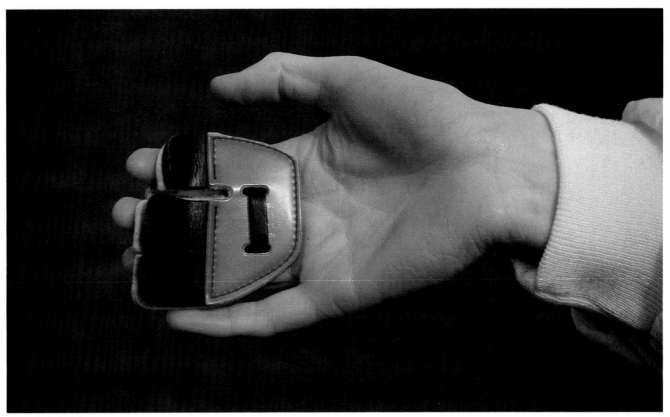

▲ *A standard finger tab*

▲ *An adjustable tab*

▲ *A belt quiver*

# Arrows

To describe the arrow we can start at the point, or *pyle*. *Pyle* is one of several old Saxon words still in use today. From the pyle the *shaft* leads to the *fletchings*. These can be shaped feathers, or more modern, plastic vanes, and serve to guide the arrow on its flight.

At the opposite end from the pyle is the arrow *nock*. This is usually a plastic moulding, fitted to the shaft, with a slot in it which enables the shaft to be fixed onto the nocking point on the bowstring. Between the pyle and the fletchings on the shaft there are ornamental rings of colours called the *cresting*.

Arrows are usually sold in sets of eight, and these sets are matched in terms of weight and spine rating. *Spine rating* is the amount the arrow shaft will bend under a given load, that load being the amount of force applied when the drawn bow is released. These factors are important for accurate shooting.

For the beginner, the most important factor is the length of the arrow shaft. This must be such that, when the bow is drawn by the archer to his natural draw length, the shaft cannot be drawn inside the bow. This would be extremely dangerous. On the other hand, the arrow should not be too long so that it overhangs the bow in front, because that would detract from the peak performance of the bow.

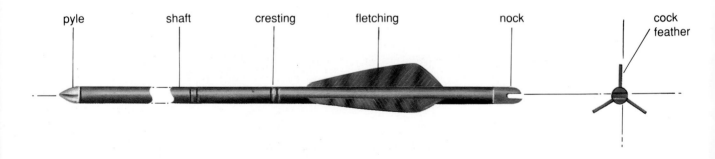

▲ *Fig. 1  The composition of an arrow showing (right) the position of the cock feather for shooting*

## Arrow materials

Arrows can be made of wood, aluminium alloy, or glass or carbon fibre.

Being of a natural fibre, wooden arrows are usually cheaper. However, they require more care and expertise in matching for shooting and keeping them safe to use. If proper care is not exercised they can become extremely dangerous to the user.

Aluminium alloy tubing, specially treated to make it tough, is the most popular arrow material, and arrows made from this are graded in quality for sale over quite a wide price range.

Glass-fibre-tube arrows are fairly durable, but are not easily matched as sets for highly competitive shooting.

Carbon-fibre tubing is the latest innovation in arrow material. It is very expensive, and it is debatable whether its performance is greatly superior to that of aluminium alloy.

▲ *Checking for arrow length*

## Types of arrow

There are many different types of arrow, some of which are illustrated in the photograph opposite.

At the top is a *fru-fru* arrow fitted with a blunt. Such an arrow would be used for shooting upwards; for instance, at something in a tree. The blunt gives a hard blow but prevents the arrow from

▼ *Fig. 2  A safe arrow length*

(a)

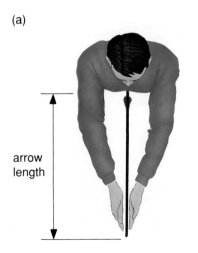

arrow
length

(b)

arrow length

sticking in. The fru-fru has so much drag in the air that it descends safely at a very low speed. For this reason it is the only type of arrow that can be shot into the air. It is more a novelty arrow than anything else.

Some archers prefer that their arrow be fletched in plastic, rather than in the usual turkey feathers. It is true that this type of arrow is more resistant to rain, but experience is needed to shoot it successfully. Below the fru-fru is a metal arrow fitted with a blunt. Target arrows are similar to this, but have a pyle fitted which may be of the bullet-nosed, ogive or chisel-point type.

Below this is a field arrow made of cedar wood and fitted with a field pyle. The arrow has a hardwood foot to strengthen it against impact damage. Such arrows are used by archers who want as accurate and strong an arrow as possible without departing from traditional materials. They should not be confused with beginners' wooden arrows, which are not footed.

Because field shooting takes place in rough countryside, many archers use low-priced wooden arrows. Experts may use aluminium arrows which are more accurate; a few even use arrows made from glass fibre.

10

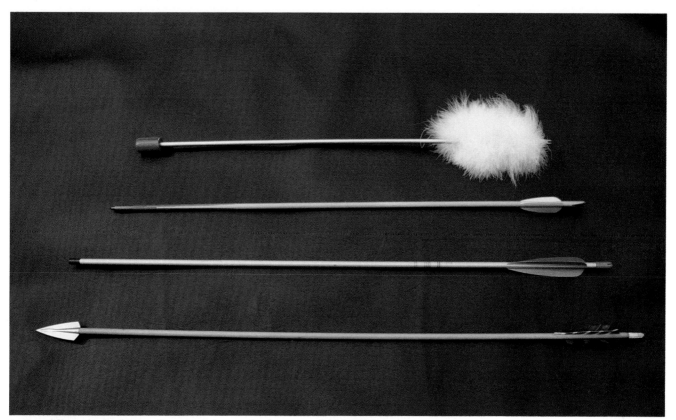

▲ *Four different kinds of arrow. From top to bottom: fru-fru; target; field; hunting*

# The bow

Archery bows all have the same basic features: a handle, and an upper and lower limb each with a groove known as the *nock* into which the bowstring fits.

## Types of bow

There are six different types of bow currently available in the shops.

The traditional *longbow* is made of wood and is usually fitted with ornate horn nocks.

The ordinary beginners' bow, usually made of lemonwood, has flat limbs. Although it serves its purpose, it has a poor ratio of energy delivered to weight pulled. The other beginners' bow is made of solid glass fibre. This performs better and is far more robust; it is therefore more popular as a club bow for beginners.

The *composite* bow is the most popular archery bow, because its design incorporates limbs which are made of laminated wood and flat fibreglass strips glued together. Some also incorporate carbon fibre in the laminations. These bows are available in two categories: the *one-piece*, which, in common with all the above, has handle and limbs joined together during manufacture; and the *take-down*, which has limbs bolted onto the handle. This allows the archer to use various limb pairs and therefore different draw weights with the same handle. When you have found a handle shape that suits you, this can prove very important.

The *crossbow* is merely a composite bow fitted to a stock, which is then operated like a rifle. The technique required to shoot from such a bow provides no challenge in terms of accuracy at short range, and therefore is of very limited interest amongst serious archers.

*Fig. 3 The composition of a simple bow* ▶

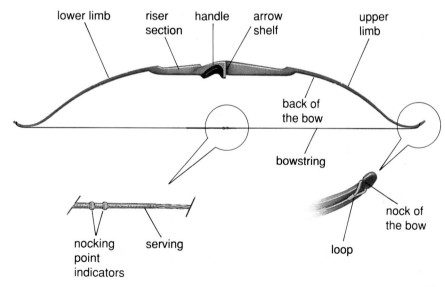

13

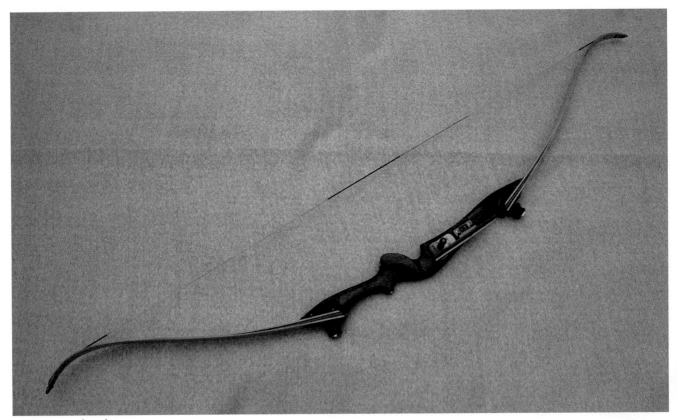

▲ *A target archery bow*

14

The *compound* bow is the latest innovation in bow design and takes into account all the laws of mechanics which have to be applied in bow design. It therefore gives maximum performance for the weight drawn. It has a handle similar to that of the composite bow, but has very short, powerful limbs to which are attached pulley wheels. To the purist, it may look like an abomination; but its performance is superior to that of any other design. The draw weight and length are adjustable within certain limitations, making it very versatile.

## The bowstring

Bowstrings are usually manufactured from a man-made fibre, of which the two most popular are *Dacron* and *Kevlar*. Longbow enthusiasts still retain the linen-thread materials; however, man-made fibres are stronger and possess other qualities which make them preferable – for example, they do not need to be treated with beeswax to make them waterproof.

The most common type of bowstring has a loop at either end to fit the nocks on the bow. The centre of the bowstring has another thread wound around it over a short distance. This thread is called the *serving*. On the serving is marked the position at which the archer places the arrow nock when preparing to shoot. This position is called the *nocking point*.

The bowstring is made to a specific length for the particular bow, so that when the bow is strung for use the distance between the bowstring and the bow is a predetermined length. This distance is known as the *fistmele* (another old term, pronounced *fist-meelee*), or the *bracing height*. This measurement is very important and is specific to the bow, the arrows being used, and the individual archer.

## Draw weight

Bows are designed and sold in various categories. Amongst other things, the description gives the *draw weight*. This is defined as the amount of effort required to pull the bow back to its *draw length*. You might see the following in a catalogue: *38 lb at 26 in*; or *30 lb at 24 in*. It is important that this information is used correctly, and this is why you are strongly urged to obtain advice from a qualified coach before beginning to use archery equipment.

When you are ready, you can buy a set of equipment, new, for around £100 (at the time of writing), which will be suitable to carry you into a high standard of shooting. Do not fall into the trap of believing that the more impressive your equipment looks, the better you will shoot.

NEVER use or purchase a bow that you cannot pull back comfortably, in the belief that you will 'get used to it' or 'train yourself to use it'. This is a recipe for disaster.

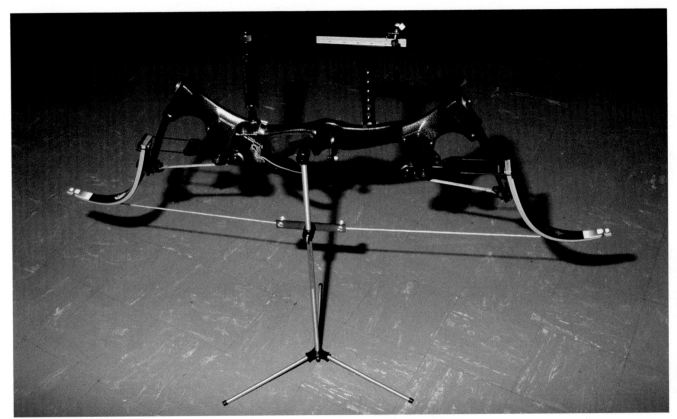

▲ *A compound bow on a stand*

# Getting started

## Clothing

Accepted dress regulations do exist, but these are not applicable to beginners. You need to ensure that you wear fairly close-fitting clothing on the upper body and arms, so that the bowstring does not catch in it during shooting.

Footwear should be suitable for the prevailing conditions. You may find that in indoor shooting ranges outdoor shoes are prohibited.

## Stringing the bow

You are strongly urged to learn to use archery equipment at a club, and not to go it alone. Do not attempt to string or unstring a bow until you have been properly instructed and given direct permission to do so. This is for your own safety as well as the safety of others.

You will find that, when stringing a bow, the coach usually does it in one of two ways. The easiest is with the

*Preparing to string the bow* ▶

▲ *Stringing the bow*

*bowstringer*, a cord with padded loops and cups used to hold the bow limbs in place. The photograph shows this in use. The pressure on the foot of the bowstringer causes the limbs of the bow to flex, so that the string can be placed in position on the bow nocks.

The other way is to put the upper loop over the upper limb on the lower limb nock, ensuring that it is correctly in place. The lower limb end is then placed in the instep of the foot, and the handle is gripped by the hand of the same side. The opposite hand is placed palm down on the upper limb by the string loop. Positioning the shoulder so that if the bow slips it cannot strike the face, the coach pulls the bow at the handle and pushes with the hand on the upper limb, sliding the string gently on the nock and ensuring that it is perfectly located.

The bow is then lifted up by the hand on the handle, and the string location is checked for correct fitting but kept well away from the face. If the string were not correctly located it could easily jump off the bow nocks and cause a very serious injury.

*Don't handle equipment without the permission of the person in charge of it.*

# Safety

Archery equipment is safe if properly used and treated with great respect. The basic rules of safety are as follows:

- never load an arrow into the bow unless you are on the shooting line;
- never draw a loaded bow except in the direction of the target;
- never shoot an arrow until the Field Captain (the person in charge of the shooting range) has signalled permission to start, usually by a whistle;
- never go in front of the shooting line until the Field Captain has signalled permission – he will only do this after he has ensured that everybody has finished shooting;
- never interfere with any equipment that does not belong to you.

# The correct way to shoot

The action of archery shooting has a common basis of style and technique, whether you choose target archery, field archery or one of the other available variations. I will discuss target archery here; any small differences between this and other forms of archery will become apparent as you try them.

On every archery range there is a shooting area and a set distance to the target area. The shooting area will have a line called the *shooting line* marked on it. Behind this is the *waiting area* where everyone who is not shooting must stand to keep clear of those who are. This is an obvious safety factor.

Each archer has a bow of a draw weight to suit him, arrows of a length which is safe for him, and an arm guard and finger tab. If you are normally right handed, you hold the bow in your left hand. The arm guard is fitted to the left forearm, and the finger tab fitted on to the first fingers of the right or drawing hand. If you are normally left handed, then 'reverse' all these accordingly.

On the starting signal, stand astride the shooting line with your feet about shoulder-width apart and your toes in line with the target at which you are shooting.

## Nocking the arrow

With the bow in your left hand and an arrow in your right hand, raise the bow to hip height, turning it so that the string is parallel with the shooting line and nearest to you, and the bow is pointing towards the target.

Determine which is the cock feather on the arrow, i.e. the one which is of a different colour from the other two. Lay the arrow down on to the bow with the cock feather uppermost, so that when the arrow is shot the other feathers do not interfere with its flight as they pass the bow. The cock feather will be at right angles to the string and outside the bow.

Push the arrow nock on to the string at the nocking point, and make sure that the string is fully bedded into the slot.

Position the arrow on the arrow rest on the bow handle, and leave it. Do not put a finger on the arrow to hold it in position.

(a)

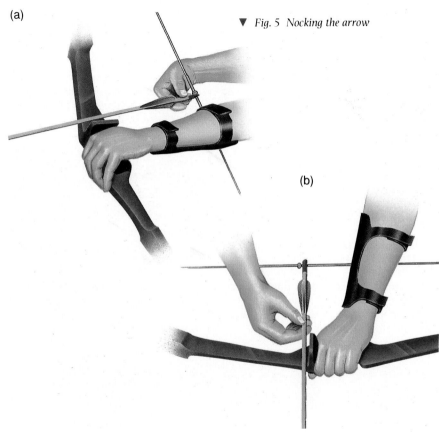

▼ *Fig. 5  Nocking the arrow*

(b)

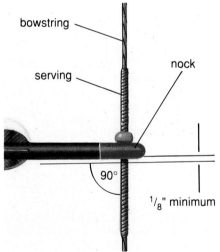

▲ *Fig. 4  The nocking point*

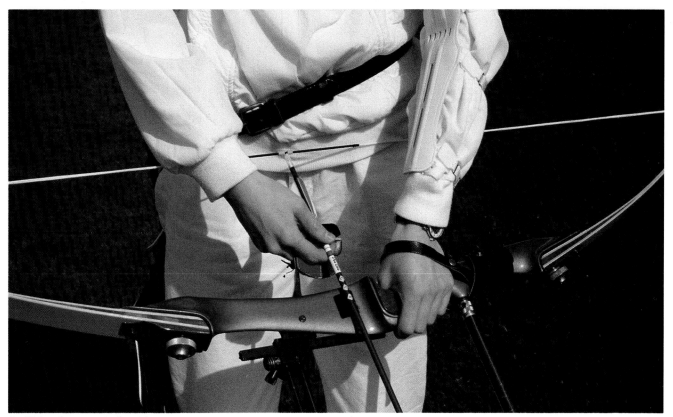

▲ *Fitting the arrow to the string*

# Hooking the string

With the finger tab in position, bring up the right hand until parallel with the string. Place the index finger under the string to the right of the arrow, and

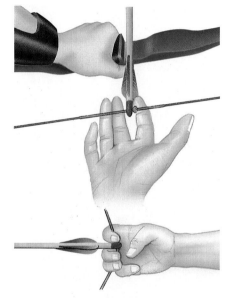

▲ *Fig. 6 The correct position of the fingers on the string when drawing the bow*

the second and third fingers to the left of the arrow. Position the string in the first joints of the fingers, and bend the tips of the fingers slightly so that you can pull the string with just the tips. The finger tab should be between the fingers and the string, and neither fingers nor tab should be touching the arrow. The arrow nock is designed to ensure that the arrow does not fall off the string.

The palm of the hand should be parallel with the string. The fingers should be straight except for the tips, which are bent around the string.

The bow is held lightly in the fork of the thumb and index finger of the left hand. The index finger is curled loosely around the bow to stop it from jumping forward on the release.

Make sure that your hips are in line with your feet, and your shoulders in line with your hips. Head erect, close your left eye and place your teeth together – but not clamped tight. Turn your head slowly towards the target until you can just see the centre of the target over the bridge of your nose; when this comes into view, stop.

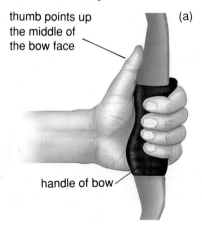

thumb points up the middle of the bow face

handle of bow

(a)

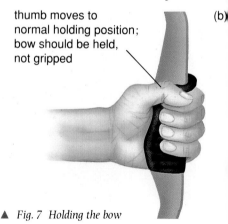

thumb moves to normal holding position; bow should be held, not gripped

(b)

▲ *Fig. 7 Holding the bow*

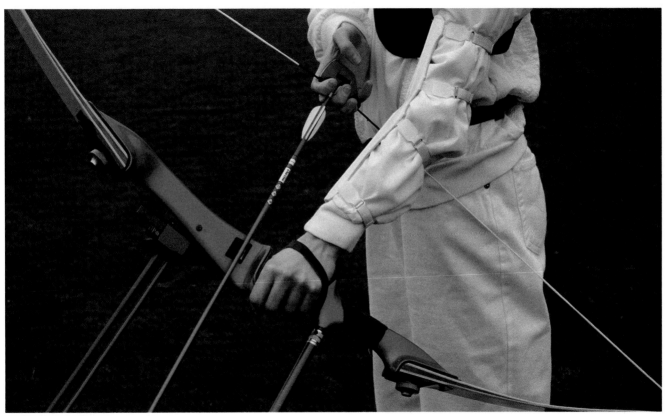

▲ *Hooking the fingers*

## The draw

Push your left hand forwards and, at the same time, draw your right hand backwards. Bring your right hand under your chin and allow the string lightly to touch the centre of your chin.

Your bow arm should be relaxed but not bent, with the elbow turned slightly outwards. The shoulder of the bow arm should also be relaxed, and not hunched.

▲ *Preparing to draw (i)*

▲ *Preparing to draw (ii)*

24

▲ *Anchoring the arrow (platform tab)*

## Taking aim

The bowsight, which will already have been set to the distance over which you are shooting, should be laid on the target. In doing this, move only your bow arm and not your head. Gently press forwards as if trying to press the sight into the centre of the target, but do not stretch your arm or hunch your shoulder.

*Aim* ▶

25

# Loosing the string

When you are satisfied that the sight is on the mark and steady, loose the string. Do this by slowly and gently relaxing your fingers around the string. The string will go forwards and the arrow will leave it.

If you have positioned your arm properly, the string will pass by your forearm and come to rest near the bracer. If you did not turn your elbow out slightly, the string may have struck your arm or the arm guard and knocked the arrow from its true flight – and possibly bruised your arm. This is why you need a coach with you to guide your first movements.

If you have balanced the gentle push into the bow and the pull of the string hand to go forward towards the target as the arrow goes into flight, and the string hand to come back as the weight is released. Retain that position until the arrow has struck the target.

▲ *Aim*

*The follow-through* ▶

# Summary

The shooting sequence as described may be summarised in the following way.

- Stand
- Nock
- Hook — fingers around the string
- Look — towards the target, do not tilt your head
- Draw — string back to the chin, bow forward
- Aim — sight on target
- Loose — (relax fingers off the string)
- Follow through — (maintain position until the arrow strikes)

You will perform this same shooting sequence throughout the whole of your archery life. With practice, it will become a skilled sequence of actions. Roger Ascham, who taught the first Queen Elizabeth the skills of archery, listed this sequence in his book on the subject, the first of many. Nothing has really changed. It is only the degree of dedication which separates the club archer from the Olympic champion and distinguishes all the levels of skill in between.

There are no short cuts. If you try to change this sequence in any way, you will find yourself paying the penalty.

# Helping yourself

So far, all the shooting advice that has been given has comprised a basic explanation of technique while working with a coach. However, there will be times when you will be practising in the club without a coach by your side. This is where life can become difficult, primarily because we tend to believe that we know exactly what we are doing and how we are doing it. This is the first error, from which all others grow.

This is easy to illustrate. Tell someone: 'Stand up straight!' It is likely that their idea of standing straight does not correspond to yours. Perhaps they are leaning forward or bending their spine unnecessarily; likewise, if you tried the same exercise, you might find that you had to make several adjustments before you were evenly balanced with a straight spine. The important thing is to ensure that there is no unnecessary tension in your muscles.

All performers practise their movements until they can carry them out correctly. Theatrical performers try out movements in front of a mirror or in the presence of a director. Sportsmen usually have a coach or some other observer who can give objective advice.

The point of all this is to emphasise the importance of using only the essential muscles, and that only after you have exercised sufficiently to warm them up and therefore avoid strain and possible injury. When you are shooting on your own, bear this in mind and do not drive yourself frantic if things do not go quite right!

# Checking the basic sequence

You are having problems in hitting the target – or the centre of the target! Always think back to the eight points itemised on page 28. Check the list through thoroughly and repeatedly. The following may help you to identify any weaknesses in your technique.

## Stand

You are standing at the shooting line, with your equipment in good shooting order. Place an arrow across the line so that it points to your target.

Now stand astride the line with your feet shoulder-width apart and your toes just touching the arrow you have positioned. Make sure that you are upright, with your weight balanced evenly on each leg without any tension in your leg muscles. In other words, relax. Your bow-arm shoulder should be pointing towards the target, and you should be looking straight ahead down the shooting line. You are now ready to begin the shooting sequence.

## Nock

Having set your feet and body correctly, nock an arrow on the string. Hook your fingers around the string, taking it in the first joints with the index finger above the arrow and the second and third below it.

## Look

Stand straight, with your head erect, and look down the shooting line. Close your teeth together, but do not clench them. Close the eye nearest the target (left if you have the bow in your left hand, and right if you have the bow in your right hand).

Turn your head slowly (without tilting it) towards the target until you can just see the gold or centre of the target over the bridge of your nose. Then stop.

## Draw

Maintain this position while drawing the bow by pulling the string back with one arm and extending your bow arm towards the target – a sort of 'push and pull' exercise. It is of paramount importance that you do this correctly.

You should pull the string by pulling your elbow up and round so that it is level with your shoulder, while at the same time pushing your bow arm forward from the wrist. Make sure that you do not over-extend your shoulder. Bring your string hand up to your chin, lightly touching your chin with the outside of the index-finger knuckle, and gently touch the string into the centre of your chin. This string and chin contact is known as the *anchor point*.

You should now have achieved an upright body position, with your head erect and turned towards the target, and positioned by your vision of the gold. The bow arm is extended but not stretched towards the target. The string arm is parallel with the arrow, hand in

◀ *A correct preparation is essential to accurate and consistent shooting*

gentle contact with the chin and elbow level with the shoulder. The weight of the drawn bow is almost completely supported by tension between the shoulder blades.

# Aim

With your body position established as above, you will find that the bowsight is on the target at which you are shooting. All you have to do now is to settle the bowsight on the centre of the target (the gold). Here we come to a very important tip which may help you turn a sloppy and inaccurate shot into a reasonable one. Choose your sighting spot on the gold; when you have your sight aimed at it, push your bow hand gently forward to the target. Avoid stretching your shoulder. Loose the string.

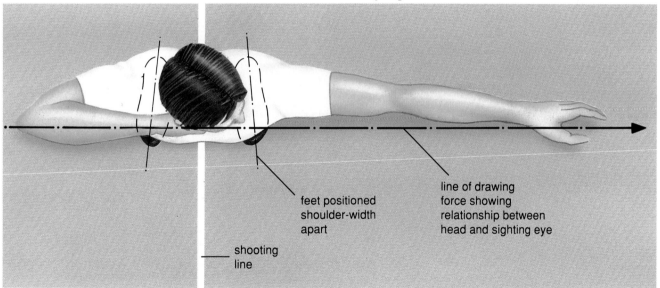

feet positioned
shoulder-width
apart

line of drawing
force showing
relationship between
head and sighting eye

shooting
line

▲ *Fig. 8  Stance of a right-handed archer when the bow is drawn*

▲ *Showing the bowsight on the gold of the target*

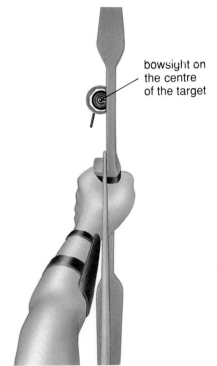

bowsight on
the centre
of the target

▲ *Fig. 9 Archer's eye view, with the sight on the centre of the target. Note that the arrow is below the target to compensate for flight parabola*

# Loose

Loose the string by gently pulling your string-arm elbow back, while at the same time allowing your fingers to straighten. This will maintain string contact with the chin until the arrow flies off it. The movement of loosing should be slow and smooth. When the string goes, it should go almost unnoticed.

As the arrow starts to move forward, the bow-arm reaction will be one of forwards movement too because of the gentle pressure you have applied. This will have the effect of helping to direct the arrow straight at the mark.

# Follow through

Maintain the body position established at the time of the loose until the arrow has struck the target. This helps you to avoid any anticipatory twitch.

After the arrow has struck, relax by lowering your arms to your sides and deliberately relaxing every part of your body – without falling over!

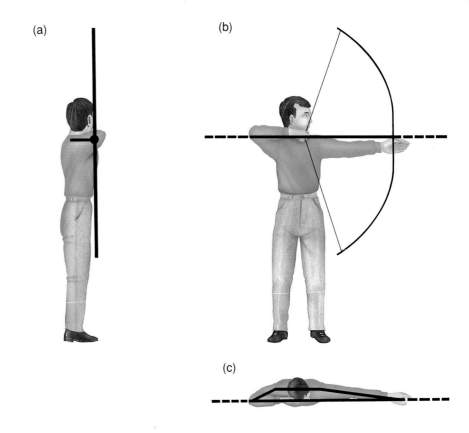

▲ *Fig. 10  Archer's stance when bow is drawn (from the front, the side and from above)*

You will need to follow the same procedure for every shot you make if you wish to achieve a consistent and accurate performance. The trick is to minimise physical and mental effort so that unused resources are available if required. Or, to put it another way, give yourself as little as possible to do, so that you have plenty in reserve.

◀ *Field archery – preparing to shoot*

*Showing the 'face walk'* ▶

# Identifying errors

As you practise your technique to the point at which you are making as few mistakes as possible, you are developing a skill. While you are doing this, make sure that you are not incorporating mistakes into that skill. It is just as easy to practise errors as it is to practise correct movements. Do not copy others until you are sure that their actions are correct: you may well be learning their mistakes. Once learned, such things are difficult to unlearn.

When errors do creep in to a reasonable shooting technique, how can you identify and eliminate them?

First and foremost, you will have realised that every time you shoot, your arrow will strike at the exact spot which was targeted by the sight pin at the time of the loose. Therefore, it is obviously important to make sure that the sight is on the correct mark when the arrow goes. What is the correct mark?

The correct mark is the place on to which you want to sight every time you aim. The easiest way to define this spot is to imagine that the outside of the gold is marked off with 'hours', like a clock face. Choose which hour-mark you find easiest, and stay with it. Lay your sight on that spot every time. Random aiming gives random results.

## Horizontal patterning

If your arrows are striking the target in a horizontally splayed pattern, it could be due to your bow-arm reaction on loosing. The best cure for this is to ensure that you exert a gentle pressure into the bow on loosing, remembering not to hunch your shoulder or lock your elbow. There must be enough flexibility in the shoulder and arm to allow a slight forward movement towards the target of the bow hand on loosing.

Alternatively, horizontal patterning may be caused by the bow position in the hand. It is important to ensure that the bow is settled centrally in the hand when you nock the arrow on the string. As you take the string onto your fingers, position the bow in the hand so that an imaginary line down the centre of the bow limb is centred into the bottom of the 'V' of the thumb and index finger bones nearest to the wrist. Settle the fleshy part of that joint into the deepest part of the handle form and keep the wrist in line with the forearm. If you do not position the bow correctly in this way, it will twist into the hand as you draw the string back. At the time of loosing the bow will then be forced back by the recovery of the twisted flesh of the palm, and this will deflect the arrow during the initial stage of its flight.

## Vertical patterning

If the pattern of your arrows on the target is 'up and down' rather than 'sideways', you could be doing one of several things wrong. Are you sure that your head is coming round to the same position each time you look towards the target to draw? If you raise or lower your head at any time, that could be the

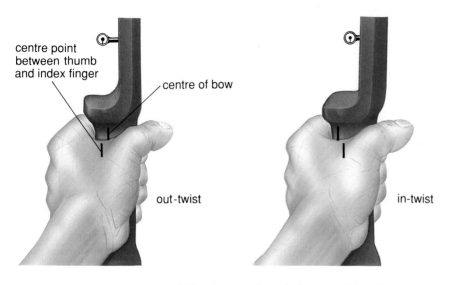

centre point
between thumb
and index finger

centre of bow

out-twist

in-twist

zero torque

▲ *Fig. 11 Bow torque. Zero torque (c) lets the arrow leave the bow smoothly and consistently*

cause. Do you always keep your teeth together while drawing and loosing?

If you are sure that these are not the reasons for the vertical arrow patterning, perhaps the problem lies with your bow hand. As you take the string on to your fingers and draw the bow gently into your hand, you should close the index finger of your bow hand around the bow, very gently – just enough to stop it from jumping out of your hand when you loose the string. Do not grip the bow tightly.

Alternatively, you may be holding the bow handle too deep into the heel of your hand. In other words, perhaps you are relaxing your wrist and so allowing too much of the bow handle to contact your hand near the wrist. The lower you are on the bow handle, the higher the arrows will fly. Try to have as little contact with the bow handle as possible, and let that be between the thumb and forefinger. It is worth noting that you are more likely to exhibit this particular fault as you get tired.

▲ *Target archery – a sport for all ages and both sexes*

# Forms of archery

There are several different forms of archery, of which target archery is the most popular. The shooting method varies slightly between the different forms.

## Target archery

Target archery is both an outdoor and an indoor sport.

Shooting is organised so that you shoot a set number of arrows at specified distances: for example, six dozen at 100 yards, four dozen at 80 yards and two dozen at 60 yards. This particular round is known as a *York round* and is usually specified for men. Women shoot a *Hereford round*, which is regarded as an equally competitive challenge but which covers shorter distances because in general women are not quite as strong as men. The Hereford round consists of six dozen arrows at 80 yards, four dozen at 60 yards and two dozen at 50 yards.

These rounds are championship tournament rounds and comprise the greatest number of arrows shot over the longest distances. There are a great number of different rounds, of·varying distances and number of arrows, listed in the rule book. The 'lowest' consists of 30 arrows at 18 yards. There are also metric distance rounds to accommodate international competitions; in these, the number of arrows to be shot equates very closely with those in British rounds.

Before the start of a round it is usual for six non-scoring arrows to be shot, in order to assist with sighting. Rules specify that you shoot arrows in groups of three consecutively.

Targets for British rounds are divided into five colour zones: the centre or gold scores 9; red scores 7; blue scores 5; black scores 3; and the outer ring, white, scores 1.

Target colours for international or metric rounds are the same, but each colour is divided into two by a thin black ring. The scoring is then as follows: inner gold, 10; outer gold, 9; inner red, 8; outer red, 7; and so on. Outer white scores 1.

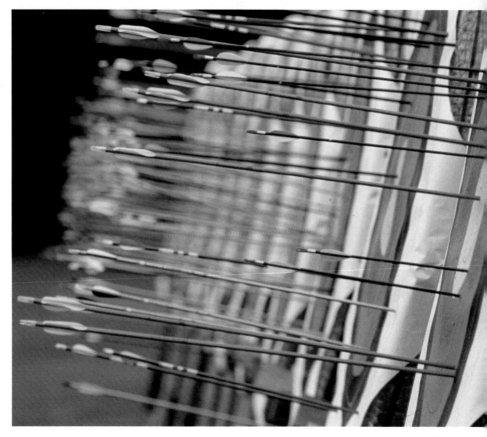

# Field archery

Field archery is very popular. Although the method of shooting follows roughly the same pattern as in target archery, it offers quite a different challenge. A field archery course is laid out over rough terrain and the targets are set up at non-specified distances within certain limits set by the rules. The targets are of different diameters and have scoring rings of a size also specified in the rules. There are two types of round: British and metric.

# Clout shooting

This is a very old form of archery derived from ancient military practice. It takes place over a maximum distance of 180 yards for men and 140 yards for women.

The target is the *clout*, which is a small flag on a smooth vertical stick, set as close to the ground as possible. This forms the centre point of the scoring area, which is sometimes marked out and sometimes determined by a non-stretch tape that is pivoted around the clout stick.

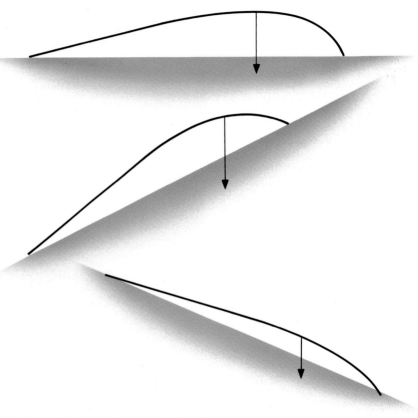

▲ *Fig. 12  Flight paths of an arrow (field archery)*

The score is determined by the distance of each arrow from the clout stick up to a maximum radius of 12 feet. Arrows entering the ground within an 18-inch radius of the stick score highest: 5 points. Those up to 3 feet score 4, and so on at 3-feet intervals, the score reducing through 5, 4, 3, 2, 1 as the radius increases.

## Flight shooting

This consists simply of shooting an arrow over the longest possible distance.

Ordinary target equipment can be used, but the real enthusiast uses short-limbed and very powerful bows, with arrows specially designed to give the least possible air resistance while in flight. To overcome any possible disparity in equipment performance for competition, different classes are nominated for different types of equipment.

At the time of writing, the world record holder is Britain's Alan Webster, who shot a distance of 1,086 yards (993.32 metres) in the unlimited class.

## Archery darts

Archery darts is extremely popular, especially in the winter months. Matches are frequently arranged with ordinary darts teams. The archery darts face has a diameter of 2 ft 6 in and is marked off like an ordinary darts board.

Shooting is over 15 yards; the ordinary darts players throw over their normal distance at a standard darts board.

## Archery golf

This is another fascinating deviation from standard archery, and takes place over an ordinary golf course – usually against golfers. You shoot an arrow from the tee, and then subsequent arrows from where the previous one landed. You hole out by hitting a 4-inch diameter disc placed level with the hole and within the green area. Each shot counts as a stroke.

This is in fact more difficult than it sounds, but it can produce a very exciting match.

## Popinjay shooting

Popinjay shooting is a very ancient form of archery, still popular on the Continent. The cock, hens and chicks are bunches of plumage, identified by different colours and arranged on perches of different heights. The cock, being at the greatest height of 90 ft from the ground, is the most resplendent.

The archer stands in an area at the base of the mast holding the birds, and shoots upwards at them. The general idea is to dislodge the birds from the perch. The scoring is 5 points for the cock, 3 for a hen and 1 for a chick.

Quite obviously, since you are shooting upwards at a target of such a height, stringent safety regulations apply. Only arrows with a blunt head are used, as shown on page 11.

# Major competitions

Archery is an Olympic sport. There are also international competitions and World Championships. Every week there is a major tournament held within 50 miles of where you live. County and regional representative teams are sent to all the major events.

Who knows, you may be one of those whose name is to be written into the team list. Or you may be one of those who enjoy archery for its own sake, for the sheer joy of shooting an arrow accurately to the mark.

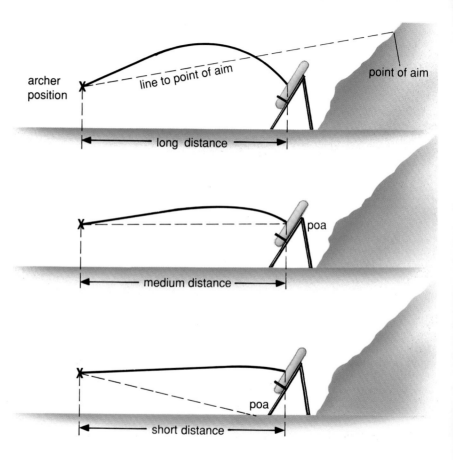

archer position

line to point of aim

point of aim

long distance

poa

medium distance

poa

short distance

*Fig. 13  Line to the archer's point of aim* ▶
*at varying distances from the target*

# Nutrition

Good nutrition is an important factor in any sport. A healthy balance of carbohydrates, protein and fat is necessary for optimum performance, in archery as in the more explosive types of activity.

Archery competitions may take place over several days, and it is therefore important to have sufficient energy 'stores' in the muscles to last over this period of time. Energy is stored in the muscles as *glycogen*. A high muscle-glycogen content is essential for endurance-type sports; explosive sports, such as sprinting and discus or javelin throwing, require a more immediate 'rush' of energy, and this can be met by foods which have a high sugar content. These foods are not suitable for archery, however, because the energy rush is followed by a drop in blood-sugar levels and consequently by fatigue.

On average, during explosive sports, an athlete requires about 450–500 Calories per hour. Archers, on the other hand, require only 250–300 Calories per hour, but their energy stores must be topped up and maintained throughout training or competition. Eat plenty of carbohydrate (bread, pasta, rice, potatoes) and keep your fat and sugar intake low.

In addition, during exercise you will perspire in order to keep your body temperature down. During this process you lose essential body fluids, which must be replaced if you are to avoid dehydration. The best thing you can drink is good plain water (not iced, just cool). If you are competing, don't wait until you are thirsty before you drink: by then, you will have dehydrated.

Above all, achieve a good balance of nutrients and fluids. Balance your intake with your expenditure. Keep your glycogen stores topped up and remain poised for action by studying your diet.

Although archery is not generally considered to be a highly energetic activity, consider this: if you use a bow of draw weight 36 lb, and shoot in a tournament requiring 144 shots (plus the six 'sighters'), you have pulled a total of 2.4 tons during the day.

Take informed advice if you are not sure of the best diet for your sport.

# Vision and sighting

When aiming the bow at the target, we use a sighting device on the bow so that we have a fixed point from which we can make changes to our body position. This enables us to cause the arrow to hit the desired mark.

Because the eye cannot focus on two objects at different distances at the same time, when looking through the sight at the target it is perhaps better to concentrate on the target and decide on the spot at which to aim the out-of-focus sighting device. Experience will help you decide on which type of sight you think you can register most clearly in your overall mental picture of both sight and target simultaneously.

For people who wear spectacles, it should be noted that the focal centre of the spectacles is usually in the centre of the lens. When you are sighting in the bow, your vision is directed to one side. This may detract from the objective of the lens prescribed. If you wish, you can obtain special lenses to give you maximum vision in the sighting position.

Archery coaches will arrange for foot markers and tactile aids to help those with sight deficiencies.

Some mention should also be made of the effects of temperature refraction. When the atmospheric temperature rises it causes the air to move, and the moisture in the air gives the impression that the object is not in the position originally observed. This is commonly known as the *mirage* effect, and is more apparent on sloping ground when temperatures are above 15 degrees Celsius. You can check for the mirage effect by positioning a sighting telescope on the target early in the morning and checking if its position appears to change during the day. Adjustments to your sighting mark (target and bow) can be made to accommodate any variations as the daily temperature changes.

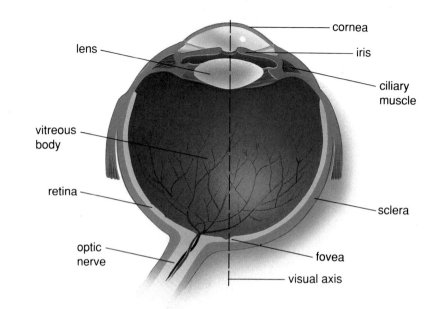

▲ *Fig. 14 Horizontal section through the eye*

# Conclusion

In order to shoot successfully, you must positively accept the necessity of choosing one particular spot – no larger than about 1 in in diameter, or 25 mm – on the target at which to aim. Larger than that, and your shots will wander all around the target. Concentration on the job in hand, and a comprehension of what that entails, will result in satisfaction.

Remember these golden rules.

● Never use a bow that is too heavy for you to pull easily.

● Always use arrows which are the correct length for you.

● Always loosen up your muscles before you are going to work them, especially the muscles of the upper torso. Keep them loose, otherwise you risk strains or even more serious muscle injury.

● Archery is a skill which has to be learned. There are no short cuts.

● Always practise on a short range, unless you also like walking. A bad shot over a short distance looks better than a bad shot over a long distance.

● Properly carried out, archery is safe and fun. Let us keep it that way.

Remember – a skill is the ability to achieve an objective. In sport, the objectives are already set ... but not the limitations.

# Glossary of terms

**Anchor point:** a constant position on the archer's face to which the loosing hand and string are drawn.

**Archer's paradox:** the apparent peculiarity observed when the arrow flexes in flight from the loose, yet an accurate shot is obtained.

**Arrow rest:** a shelf on which the arrow rests during the draw, located just above the bow handle.

**Arrow shelf:** *see* arrow rest.

**Barebow:** shooting without a sight fitted to the bow.

**Belly of the bow:** the face of the bow which is on the same side as the string.

**Bodkin:** a long, square, tapered pyle, historically used for piercing knights' armour.

**Bolt:** short arrow for use with a crossbow.

**Boss:** target, usually made of compressed straw.

**Bouncer:** an arrow which hits the target and rebounds from it.

**Butt:** a target boss which is permanently erected, usually of straw bales or turf.

**Button:** an adjustable pressure point for the arrow to bear against while passing the bow.

**Cast:** a term used to described the ability of a bow to project an arrow.

**Creeping:** allowing the arrow to move forward from full draw before being loosed.

**Cresting:** bands of colour painted around the arrow for decoration or identification.

**Draw-force line:** an imaginary line through the bow arm to the elbow of the drawing arm.

**End:** the number of arrows required to be shot in sequence.

**Fast!:** a warning cry used to stop all shooting in an emergency.

**Freestyle:** a type of field shooting which allows the use of sights.

**GMB:** Grand Master Bowman – the highest classification of bowman.

**Group:** the name for a cluster of arrows in the target.

**Hanger:** an arrow which strikes the target yet does not penetrate enough to hold it firmly (so that the arrow hangs down).

**Lady Paramount:** appointed traditionally as supreme arbiter and also to present awards and prizes.

**MB:** Master Bowman – the second highest classification of bowman.

**Overbowed:** using a bow with a draw weight which is too heavy for the archer.

**Overdraw:** to draw the pyle of the arrow inside the face of the bow.

**Perfect end:** maximum score for consecutively shot arrows according to the prevailing rules.

**Pinching:** touching the arrow with the fingers of the drawing hand.

**Pinhole:** the exact centre of the target face.

**Recurve:** the curvature of the bow limb away from the archer at the nock ends of a bow.

**Riser:** the centre section of a bow including the handle.

**Skirt:** the outer edge of the target as a non-scoring area.

**Spine:** the measured ability of an arrow to bend.

**Stabilisers:** weights added to the bow to reduce bow vibrations.

**String (endless):** corded threads wound onto a former with thread ends knotted together, having two loops formed to fit onto the bow nocks.

**String (laid-in):** corded threads with loops formed for bow nocks, the whole worked into a rope form without any knots.

**Target Captain:** person in charge of the conduct of the archers at a target.

**Target Day:** a club shoot organised in accordance with GNAS rules.

**Target face:** a cover marked with scoring zones, placed over the target boss, usually made of paper.

**Target Lieutenant:** assistant to the Target Captain.

**Target stand:** wooden stand supporting the boss.

**Timber hitch:** used to secure the bowstring when that string has only one loop.

**Toxophile:** a student of archery.

**Toxophilus:** the title of the first book on archery, written by Roger Ascham and published in 1544.

**Underbowed:** to use a bow of too light a draw weight (therefore not using your full physical potential).

**Unit aiming:** maintaining the relationship of the arms, head and shoulders by adjusting the aim from the waist.

**Vane:** plastic fletching on an arrow.

**Waiting line:** a line 5 yards behind the shooting line where archers wait while others are shooting.

# Index